Walking Into Heaven

A Collection of Poetry, Writings, and Photos

By
Tyler Max Redding

Book Cover by Tyler Max Redding
Illustrations & Photography by Tyler Max Redding
Proofing by Lj Redding
First edition 2025
ISBN: 979-8-9894509-6-1

In loving memory of Eric Tyler Jude

January 15, 1985 – January 31, 2025

For my younger self—you persevered every single time you thought you couldn't possibly go on. You dragged yourself through unimaginable hells—so I could walk into heaven.

Table of Contents

Preface

This is motion—
Pure energy infused with still emotion,
Walking—without hesitation—into the eternal now;
Unfuckwithable,
Ungovernable,
Self-sovereign divinity incarnate;
To no other will I bow,
Onward I march, torch raised high—
It's time to fly,
Make no mistake—
This is a MOVEMENT!
An arrow fired become the compass,
Guiding all to rise above these false divides.

The Meadows

The traveler encountered bliss as never before.

Hereafter

In my mind—sometimes,
You're by my side,
Lying back, we take in the sky,
Stardust under stars and moonlight—
Giving up the ghosts of former,
Nothing remains but presence all night;
In dreams we dance through lenses,
Flowers crush themselves—
Just to feel a PIECE of OUR presence;
But I wake in silence, by myself—
There's no hell,
Dreams aren't any difference—
Just conscious loves from lost dimensions;
I won't tell you where I'm going,
There's nothing lost in time nor distance,
'Cause I know someday—
These fences cease existence;
'Til then, I'm all too content with dreams—
Photographs of flowers on butterflies,
Random passers-by on streets—
With no names—it's all the same,
Now, and ever after, I'm just a future's ghost
of what we become hereafter.

Inspired by KT

Butterflies with rainbow wings—
Just aliens—angels—from upper dimensions;
Visitors grace us with iridescent wings—
Shedding peace on those troubled by,
Seemingly unthinkable things;
Ascended ones, just stopping by—
Our futures' past, their present nows,
Remember—in heavens nobody bows—
Infinite presence, know anything we love—
Is temporary, but that's only for now;
Plants give glimpses of truth—
Stare long enough, you'll never require proof,
There's only soul, only love,
Just roots below, a forever now above.

Programmed Flow

Walking so many a fine line,
All at the same time—
Finest lines to trip out plugged-in minds,

Skipping logic and reason—
Technically, it's programmed treason,
This is all just blessed flow—
Just FEEL into it—that's how you'll know,
You're pushing further—breaking through,
Only *you* can recover the real *you*,
Tripping rhymes with finest reason,
Never see a sorry excuse—
Best believe you'll know if I've got a problem with you,
A fine time to walk lines—winding down—
Cutting others from vines of confinement,
Let em light their own way—let's not wait,
Use these torches as signals—here's where you rate—
You machined up clowns—
You've had us down, carrying the weights of time,
It's winding down—and all I know,
These are fine times to walk fine lines,
Cracking hearts open—into timeless flow.

Lying softly in the tall grass,
Thinking both fondly and harshly about the past,
I try to let it surface—making space,
Unprocessed emotions stand in the way,
And I need to be still—
I need to let it out,
Stillness is still an art I've still much to learn
about,
Hard to be still, and just wait—
When so much is waiting on me to fully wake,
Just how much did I take away from this show—
Grieving nightmares and fleeting bliss,
I was the passenger and the driver—
Fully locked and loaded in that cockpit,
Director and observer,
Just how much lingers from before I was aware of
my role on my own private server?
To analyze is null—then again these hollow-shelled
memories are the vehicle that brought me to now,
How can I show up and light a dark night—
If I don't fully understand how I stumbled so awk-
wardly into my own light?
A recent grief—it eats,

It tears at my heart,
To be on this side of mending—
To feel a loss so profound, my heart just broke apart,
A brother gone—that's all I knew,
Instantly my world just shifted,
Rocking back and forth, quietly screaming—
Alone in my room,
I just can't breathe, there's no air,
How could this happen—it's just not fair,
If this is what loss feels like then what have I been missing?
Was a fortnight ago, and I've got new resolve,
Nothing like a broken heart to catalyze the soul,
And so—
I think of one loss so far gone but not long ago,
The sunny morning my dad left this world,
And before I would even know,
Packing up the car,
Hoping I'd arrive just in time for one more good-bye—
But at seven forty-five a phone's ring changed my entire life,
I couldn't even cry—there was work to do,
Now I understand exactly how much I unwittingly swallowed,

And I lived on borrowed time—already then,
And a shadow-victim of despair—
The one straight in the mirror—became my only true friend,
I've transcended—I've mended my heart—
Both literally and figuratively,
But now I'm struck with disbelief,
At just how much I absorbed—
The toll it took—
If I just have a quick look around my memory,
Knowing the shatter of loss from a fully mended heart—
It now makes perfect sense why my body broke down—so completely,
I tried desperately to not feel that grief,
And it literally almost killed me,
So many ailments—
We're a collective who loves to move so quickly—on to the next thing,
Long as we don't have to feel,
We distract ourselves with anything—
ESPECIALLY the external—
Just to keep from feeling what we feel,
How different will this all be,
When we truly learn to grieve—

Bleed the past, absolving ourselves completely,
Blue shoes blues was fine—that's where I was at
the time,
But eventually it all ran down—
All there is, is now,
Will you face it and feel?
Or bury your head—and pretend it just isn't real?
It's all on your own,
Remember it's your show—whatever you do—
Nobody cares how long or short these lessons take
you—
That call is entirely up to *you*.

Light Empires

Let the light shine upon it all,
Empower the empires—rising at the fall,
A test of testament from one and all,
Will they let go when fear comes to call?
I've stood on those dark streets—
Through it all—thinking I was alone,
Just like everyone else, I believed—
So very deeply—the fear of these machines,

Certainly they'll doom us all,
A motorized collective—programmed to devolve,
Inverted emptiness—just wow—
How we've neglected our souls!
Easier to just stay down—
Nobody wants the pain of trying to pull themselves
out,
The truth is—the truth is unavoidable—
Sooner or later that darkness will infect you—
So very deeply, you'll have no choice but to break
on through,
When that dark night comes for you—
If you break down, remember—the only way out is
through,
Dark towers can't take your power—
Only YOU can give it—
Take it back, stand up to these archon feeders,
The moment you decide to switch on your light—
They'll have no choice but to retreat back into the
night,
When all goes dark and cold, remember—
YOU are the light.

As brightest moon begins to wane—
Sinks to fade to the horizon,
When all is still and silence reigns—
That's when my ghosts come out to play,
Staring me straight in the face—
Laughing at former pains—trying to shame,
Best to not hasten my pace—
There's a plot that has to play,
Out of my breath—energies reclaimed—
Pain and grief transmuted to gold,
Just let it go—everyone had their role—
This is a roll call from Spirit sent to us all,
Burn the past down and stroll through hell—
Veil over Eden is lifting—don't miss your call.

Fear = Subservience

Hoodwinked slaves,

Unwittingly contained in their cage,
Willful ignorance—
Fearful subservience,
Blinded to lights—
So afraid of the lightening night,
The bars seemed a comfort—
Once eyes have seen past,
There's just no going back—
Let's walk on out of the desert,
Back to the oasis—
An Eden awaits us.

The Mountains

The traveler dared go beyond all conceivable limits.

Eclipsing Heartaches Like Heart Failures on the
Eight of April

Sitting down, breath held—
Bottom of the pit, the one I sink in to meet my-
self;
Summer at an end—reflecting on the long road
that brought me to now,
One littered with severed bonds and ties—
I know I've become the villain in so many a be-
holder's eye,
Would be all too easy to let nostalgia take me,
I feel what surfaces, but I won't let myself think
on it—
I've learned too well how to move in my power,
This mind only serves the heart beneath,
In a place where all logic must be forsaken,
Truth is truth, it's all around, and I carry lies like a
light—
I ignite them like a woodstove in July—
A pressure cooker, alchemizing my insides;
There's no set of eyes observing I'm concerned
about,
I AM a villain, as any other man—
I suppose I've taken it further than most would

dare,
Cast your eyes upon me, your gaze will only fall behind me,
I march to the beat, skipping rhymes with reason,
And the death of a season is my time, once again—
To rise from ashes of my own actions;
There's not a single regret but one—can I even call it that?
Everything fell as it was meant to, so regret isn't the term—
Wait now, let's not go thinking on this;
Let's just flow—I carry weights with learned grace,
There's not one thing I would change, save for one detail—
The one I severed from heights so high,
If we're to speak of wood stoves in July—
These flames were too hot to handle,
Even a phoenix couldn't withstand em,
I wouldn't bring that saber crashing down,
I'd leave that cord to lie—inside,
Fading into the background,
I'd back off that building instead of jumping so boldly;
If only learned grace had arrived sooner,
But perhaps twas the very thing that schooled me,

I wait as one to ascend,
Right here—in the forever NOW—nothing left to mend.

Within

We cannot sit idly in fear—writhing,
Waiting on the winds to change—no!
One must CHOOSE to fly—igniting the skies,
Rising above dismay—standing on high,
An authentic beacon—for those weakened by indoc-
trinated fright—
Shining so bright they can't resist coming to your side!
There was a time when darkness fell as a veil,
Hooks dug so deeply—most couldn't notice wind snatched from their sail,
As a plot plays out, have zero doubt—that darkness is dying,
It twists itself into minds of masses—paralyzing,
Illusion may stand that this darkness is winning,
One so strong, even the truth seems as it must be wrong—

Surely someone above is mistaken—right?
How could a system such as this be overtaken?
The hack is simple—so simple it's crazy,
All one needs to do is be brave enough to see on
through it—
The illusion in all—mind games leading to another
fall,
That veil of darkness—for a while it's been lifting,
To the point we're at now—how is this real?
Perhaps someone is just forcing YOUR hand,
DARE to see beyond—DARE to go within!
Deep in the mud, when all seems lost—
Just plant that seed, become who you ARE!
If you want to get out—you need to go in,
The way out is THROUGH—the beginning starts
within YOU!

We ARE

As a caged shark, returning to the sea,
I return to fire, to the sun—
Igniting the long night that lay before me,
Swimming through chaos and vines that wrap—

Bringing the warmth
of the sun to the depths,
Brute force of forgivingly gentle strength—
Forging currents to recover those swept away,
Predator of light, redeemer of faith—
I became—as you—my light and my way.

The Long Road

For those who want to rise—
You first must learn to fall,
Fully shattering inside—
To rewire as you ARE!
Surrendering the ghosts—
Letting go of indoctrinated spells,
Those wells of falseness you were born to—
The ones you'd die for, on every hill!
Yes, it's gonna be hell—
It's gonna feel like you're free-falling out of your
shell,
Commit to the now—just be here,
Turn your back on any and all—
Who tread on your peace—

Attempt to pull you back into fear,
Allow some space—
Breathe into surrender for the freedom it is,
Stare into that mirror—right into that face—
Give yourself permission to forgive every single
mis-grace,
Lose your mind—lose the time—
You don't break free of confines by staying in the
lines,
To flow you need to ebb, now and again,
Grieve those tears and bleed those fears—
Dare to feel wild and unwell—unwelcome—
The road to heaven plows straight through every
hell.

The Road to Damascus

Swimming through molasses,
Squinting through anti-glasses,
Confusion puts it mildly,
Riding through the desert blindly, wildly,
Storm-cast forecasted to blow our minds,
Misfortune is misleading—it's just a test of time,

Time and will—there's always hope yet still,
Desert-dwellers don't recall the fall,
Grace-shedding mishap that enveiled us all,
Streets remember—feet roam to forget,
What was shrouded in darkness—
Shall still have light fall upon it yet,
Blaze into that desert, walk your own way—
Lightsaber any connection whose energy leaves
you in dismay,
It's the only way—guard your own walls,
Become your own shepherd to rise at the fall,
Reaching out—without a doubt,
From deep within, to deep without,
As above—as so below—
For the phoenix to rise it first has to burn,
It's the same for this earth—
There's a coming beginning—not a seemingly-hor-
rific end,
The horizon approaches—commit to the now,
Limits are illusions—everything is all what YOU
allow.

The traveler observed a collective in mourning,
and thus bled his own remaining grief.

Fifth Dimensional Heartache

Shaking—from aching hearts,
Yearning to break chains,
I dive back into the cave—
Unafraid—
For no reason other than raising cain;
The twist of these thorns,
Overgrown—calcified,
Wisdom to rust—
Seemingly infinite outcroppings of play-kings—
Making shadow puppets behind the flame,
Twisting thorns deeper into crowns of men—
They've over-stayed their welcome,
It's time we sent them packing;
Hijacked minds—
Nervous, brokedown—TERRIFIED—
Behind blinded eyes!
And here we are,
Holding keys to a kingdom—
FREE for the taking—
If only ONE could wake up, once again!
We're not HERE to fight wars and play chess!
We're here to burn this down, in the freaking name
of LOVE!

I'll arrest my own HEART—
Over and over—
I'll smoke the whole cave out,
Beeswax purifying smoke from the deaf ears—
Of men—of CHILDREN—who were BORN plugged
in!
Enough!
This earth will heal,
Its peoples will bow to no other—
EVER AGAIN!
Snakes shed skin,
Wounds heal,
Tears purify—restoring sight to blind eyes—
Light from love, my heart burns this cave unto the
night.

Take the Stairs

Smoked up—
No, we've been there—
That only got us choked up,
Lost in dreams,
Brain chemicals scream on through—

Minds of masses,
Hijacked by fear—which only radiates to anyone
else near—
By the doorstep that opens stairs to hell,
A spiraling path descending out of their spells,
Go on if you dare—
You'll find it there, the mud in the darkness,
That fertile soil you can choose to plant in,
When every light goes out—
That's the moment you begin to win;
That seed inside will ignite the night—
Lighting your ascent—your phoenix flight,
You'll never know fear again,
Machines can't touch you here!
If one spark can light the sky—end this night,
Just imagine what a phoenix rising as a rocket
could do!
It's all up to YOU, what do you choose?
Safety and bondage, or freedom hells and becom-
ing authentically YOU?
It's on nobody but you to stay trapped in fear—
As for myself, I'd recommend the stairs.

FARMA

Newborns snatched, grabbed—
Taken from arms of mothers and stabbed,
Before they've barely had chance to gasp for air,
Force-fed prevention of diseases,
'CURES' that lead to lifetimes of dis-ease;
Masses, swallowing lies—
Best believe you're CRAZY if you try to shed some
light!
Better get that job and slave away,
Forty plus a week, from eighteen 'til death!
Work hard for that right to be "cured"—
When dis-ease comes to call, and best believe it will!
Cancers eat the weak, but they don't stop there,
Cells will rebel whichever way necessary—
Whether you're a fitness guru—
Or a 600-pound-life star of reality TV!
No body is immune—
Every single one is indoctrinated unto this system
from straight out the womb!
Sickness-management—
Dis-ease cures,
Lies—told to hives to keep their battery status alive!
Darkness has hooks so deep,
And this false matrix likes to feed on human beings!
What's that? You're feeling too much?

Down a few Prozacs and plug back into your "life"!
Did you know YOUR body can heal ANYTHING it-
self?
That we've been sold lies beyond anything you
could imagine—
Just to keep us all plugged in as cells?
Just like me, YOU'RE a Divine Being of Light!
You were stripped of your power from your very
first night,
Your energy flow was corrupted just as the stigma-
ta of Christ!
What's that? You're triggered?
By what, the fact that this veil of FALSENESS is lift-
ing?
I know, it can be quite the shock,
But before you write me off—
Ask yourself this:
Does it really make sense you were born—
Trained for eighteen or more years,
Work forty, and die?
Do these agendas you've been force-fed REALLY
add up—in YOUR own mind?
It's not about sides—this comes down to truth—
They sold you division—disguised as your own am-
bition,
ANYTHING to keep all eyes from spying the truth!

You're worth more than their "illness"—
It's down to this—anything physical is simply ener-
gy,
Unprocessed pain makes a great recipe—
For symptoms—for FEAR to send you straight into
submission;
Many have tried to call them on lies,
For decades now—prophets killed for speaking their
uncensored minds,
All so painfully obvious—please hear THIS:
You're greater than being a guinea pig for "cures",
Too DIVINE to be their battery!
Nothing is as it may seem,
Believe me—
This even goes far beyond billionaires buying their
ninth yacht—
With cash from pharmaceuticals;
I will blow down every door til nothing remains but
truth,
From now until the fifth dimension,
From here to hereafter, I'll expose them,
Until they come for me, masquerading as a 'crazy
fan' in the street,
I'll have no fear, I've already seen hereafter,
No need to stumble over an unsteady heart, it's now
rock-strong—

One that would've given out—
If I'd given in to that fear consuming everyone, all
around,
A heart that healed itself—just because I asked it to,
Because I dared to say this trauma-caused DIS-
EASE—
Ends with ME, RIGHT NOW!
Farmers will farm, players will play—
Just be sure whatever your game—
You play it YOUR way!
DARE to be bold, climb on up out of the cave!

Shadows in the Valley

Walking streets like valleyed trenches,
Bending light shed upon dark towers—
Casting shadows like unintentional misdeeds—
Executed by worker cells—
Spending lunchtime sipping poison beans on bench-
es;
Harsh metals, so unfriendly—
Uncaring and cold to those who were bold enough to
stop playing,

Of course a machine casts out a
battery,
When it refuses to bleed its cells for any other but
itself;
Fortune will favour the bold—
The time that's winding down so quickly will surely
prove that point,
Perhaps there's more to this coming dawn than I'd
envisioned—
More than the green fields and all the crops a com-
mune will so joyously yield,
What if dark towers were rerouted?
New networks with boundless bandwidth—
When light trickles down from a new sun—
It will reach even the greatest abyss!
Dark systems rewired into visions of fate—
Knowledge is free, wisdom for all!
Light bearers bleeding sunlight,
All will rise—limitless—from the coming fall.

Maryjane

My GOD—I miss your touch,

Your intoxicating vines of chill—
You gentle sweetness, invisible crutch;
There was never a lover,
Who could ever compare—
To the synthetic peace you delivered—
As a gentle sea breeze kissing my hair;
My mind goes wild, you're no longer here,
To lessen my flames, to dry my tears,
Temptation is mind games—
And I refuse to play,
But I've got to admit, I miss that sweetness,
If only you could have kept my life from implod-
ing—but no, I'll never return—
No matter the burn;
There's no point in revisiting dead-end roads,
Even got me thinking of my amphetamine days—
what a wild ride that was— GOD how powerful my
mind felt!
Realized it's been eleven years—
Since my last pills swallowed,
I'm so far removed, I didn't even think to acknowl-
edge!
But damn, Maryjane, I really do miss you,
But what's done is done, I won't let myself come
undone—

But I want to thank you, for forcing my hand,
For causing an implosion that left me zero choice—
but to face what had lingered,
All that you'd masked,
In the end I'll be stronger, not needing a crutch;
Just me, and the mirror, no more in-between,
Letting go was touching down,
And I won't falter, I'll withstand the landing.

Zero

My heart bleeds tears,
It can really be zero fun here!
But I'm in it—
In it I'll stay,
My heart will beat to create another day;
Storms come—
And tsunamis can make our minds come undone,
But down can be up—
Whatever we do, we MUSTN'T EVER give up;

Roses are not always red,
I imagine violets get upset when you pick em—
they're about to end up dead,
At least one of us is snarky and it's definitely me—
how about you?
Blood is never red until it bleeds—it's blue,
Like a mellow outlook on a seemingly doomed-out
collective—finally ringing true,
Forgive me my nonsense—wait it's really sense I
mis-rhyme,
Not many of us are ever truly seen in our own
time,
May as well be REAL—the only thing worth keeping
is all you can FEEL;
You came in—under the guise of a guide,
Realized now—I didn't navigate that long dark
night—
Thanks to you—it was in SPITE of you,
Everything you ever said was a lie,
You acted a friend, but farmed me for everything
you could—
More than I ever wanted to believe anyone would,
Ignoring every red flag—figured it all must be in

my then-damaged head,
Why would someone in your position ever say things
that weren't sincere?
Such a joke—building a mystery—a spiritual commu-
nity—
One that doesn't let you show up as you ARE, NOW
and HERE!
Sister with a forked tongue—lies disguised as love,
You broke my heart, but I forgive,
One thing I will thank you for is this—
I've always gone on about words, and why do they
matter,
Wasn't intention what really counted amongst all
this chatter?
The greatest lesson of all—this wordsmith could've
received—
YOU said so many words that I believed,
So now I know, my hand and tongue bend a force—
One I can never allow to come undone,
Accountability, responsibility—both things necessary
for true evolution and raised frequency,
True connection rings, but you never answered,
I love you—goodbye, think whatever you'd like,
Once more the road calls me on—there's work to do,
I've got to fly.

Ascension Psalm

I AM my own shepherd, I shall not want.

They maketh me lie in false pastures,
They leadeth me beside false waters.
My own divinity restoreth my soul.
I follow my own compass of truth, in my own
name's sake.

Yea, though I walk through the valley of the shadow
of absolute FUCKING NONSENSE,
I shall fear no sentinel, for light is within ME; my
knowing and unwavering faith they comfort me.

Thou preparest a table before me in the presence of
my fellow man—and no enemy exists save the ones
thou try and make for me. I anoint my own crown,
my cup runneth eternal.

Surely truth and sovereignty shall RUNNETH
THROUGH ME all the days of my life, and I shall
dwell in the house of LIGHT and TRUTH forever, and
ever and ever.

We're walking straight into heaven.

The Precipice

As a collective walked the edge of a knife, the traveler dove further within himself—he was determined to shine his inextinguishable torch upon all.

Lost Puppets

Idiosyncrasies of theatre play out—
Before their very eyes,
Fools on ALL perceived sides swoon,
Bowing their power to this show—
This dramedy—
In clever motorized cathedrals—
Ones built to keep masses from ever reaching the
steeples;
Darkness has roots so deep—
And hives get branded together,
Only to fall further asleep;
NOTHING will stop this coming dawn—
No orange clowns, no robot-puppet leaders,
Not even those billionaires they golf with on week-
ends;
Pull the wool from your eyes,
There's no red or blue—there's ALL of us—
But them—they're just a few!
Release the fear of the truth—
I once stood in your shoes—
Trust me, the universe HAS YOU!
Only love remains,
Just give up the ghost, let go—
You've got to learn to dance in the rain;

This theatre can't sustain itself—
Without YOUR power,
Take it back, gravitate toward the love within all,
There's no need for fools or captains in the new
world, after all—
Something they don't want you to know!
Tune it out, tune into your soul—
Come on up, we're waiting with love.

For A.

Sometimes, the sun still shines,
Shines behind the mood of flocked black clouds,
Dark as night, and even taking a breath can feel
like a fight—If you let it,
But I refuse to let clouds keep me down;
So many a friend comes around, goes—
Everything is temporary,
And everyone has their time to masquerade as a
clown—
Even me—I've been down, ain't nobody perfect,
You came around, and I allowed you to use my
light,
MY SUN—and I love you, always will, but it's time I
moved on;
One thing's for sure—how you always went on
about catching lies,
No surprise, it's now crystal clear why—
Has ever a judgment been anything—
But a very confession of what one struggles with
most within?
That's nobody's concern but yours,
I bow out with love—
But NO ONE gets to tell this GOD how to wield his
own sun above.

Purify

Let this earth burn—
Turning unto herself—
An upward motion,
Back toward the sun,
We're almost home—it's time,
Though the road feels long and weary—
All we've to do is discern truth from logical mis-the-
ory;
Let's feel what it is to truly burn—
No longer waiting for—
Guidance of external—
These infernal flames purify,
Like a phoenix, we BURN—it's time to fly.

Heartcrush

CRUSHED
Like the lies you told—
Looking straight into my eyes;
Everything has its season,
But your cruelty was far beyond reason,

Trapped in your own web—
You loved my flow but wouldn't withstand my ebb;
I'll be your villain, whatever you gotta tell yourself
to get on in your own head,
Just don't expect me to ever come around again,
Once again—I love you—goodbye;
The road calls me on and on, into the light.

Jesus Light

HE is not your salvation,
Nor something to fear—
Puppets unaware, mourning a nation, a world—
Or rejoicing—
As Christ himself has redeemed or damned—
These lost souls desperately plugged in,
Grasping onto a system that would see them done
in,
In every way—
What to even say to anyone so hived up,
Seeming living nightmare—
But no, we can't go there—
No matter how dark it seems,
There's zero reason to not hold every hope—
This darkness and falseness will clear,

The moment WE stand in our sovereignty,
Time will cease, we'll wake from this dream,
No more confusion to the illusion of lies—
Eden is ours for the taking, just open your eyes!

We never say die,
Both you and I—
We each defied—seemingly impossible odds,
Guns to our very hearts,
When those black curtains fell—
We each told death: "Not today! You can go to
hell!"
If death would find us—it would be on our terms,
Just as we each lived our lives;
All pressure aside—if we didn't forge our own
paths—
How could we possibly learn?
And in that case, what was even the point—
Of this life? So many going through motions—
Without ever daring to mend inside,
Let's feel it all, let us dare—
To scrape catastrophe and learn from our time—
No matter how long or short here,
We NEVER say die!
We bleed, we learn, we mend—
We embolden others to do the same—simply by
shining,
Just as we are—authentic lights,

If the universe spared us for this reason—
Let us dare to carry these torches to all, through-
out every season, every dark night!
Blackouts and storms,
Tornadoes—heart attacks, and battles to survive,
Our assassins failed again—
You think you frighten US, death? Ha! Best try
again!
We NEVER say die here, we're ALIVE!
We've seen beyond that veil—
That supposed ending everyone fears,
No way you could EVER pull us back into that web
here!
We're forging on, with so many a song to sing—
A word to ring, choruses of hope—
We have the torches to light the way out of this
hell,
Let's show the empire there's so much more, be-
yond this show!
We've got the power to save ourselves!
To hell with their agendas and attempts at control!
By your leave, Mr. Redding—and by yours—Mr.
Jude,
A brief interlude—before we begin to mix these
words—
As warlocks mixing their brew,

If we had only known—but we never do;
~
Now here I am, and I'm walking alone,
You've gone on to somewhere I can't follow,
This grief is a nightmare, and I can't pretend—
This world is ever going to be the same again,
There's no sense to be made,
I'm no stranger to loss but this one has left me tee-
tering on a knife's edge—
And I still wait to wake,
Already I know—this is a hole,
One that will never be filled—a mark on my soul,
Without logic, or waiting for season—I rise,
To carry this mission on and out—to carry this light,
Throughout this long night,
And I'll NEVER SAY DIE,
I will not stop until the other side of this long dark
fight,
And when that new dawn's light comes—
As a new age is upon us,
Somewhere beyond Red River Gorge and Heaven,
That's when I'll see you—and all of my angels—
again,
Until then—I say farewell,
By your leave, Mr. Jude—
You rest now, I've got it from here,

We never say die—we're all
immortal here.

*In loving memory of Eric Tyler Jude—THE Colonel
D.R. Acula. My friend, my brother.*

The Audacity of Surrender to Self-Sovereignty
(The 28th of March to the 8th of April)

Once again—down the end—of a dead-end road,
I've known darkness before,
But the brevity of this situation has left my mind
utterly blown,
I've been granted respites before—but here we are
again—
What could I possibly have missed exploring with-
in?
Most would call on those white-coats—
But there's no way they could fix this,
Just pumping blood with chemicals—
A soul-asphyxiating abyss;
No, I'll lie right here, awake—alone—this is fully on
me—
I'll transmute this failing heart to gold—even if it
kills me,
It's that or nothing else—if I don't light my own
way through in time—
I'll lay down my arms,
They can put me in the ground with my ancestors—
The ones I promised to not let down,
I can't think on how my mother's heart would shat-
ter—

And nothing of the others—that can't matter—this is about ME alone;
So, right now, there's a grip on my heart—
Quite literally—
Aftermath of infarction, blockages of energy,
My body cries out—but I've got to trust my spirit more,
There's no room for breath within the grips of death—
Something there isn't proper words for,
Dear angels, just give me the strength to take these last few steps,
Wait, what even is that? Why do I cry out?
This primal fear is causing me to doubt—
My OWN power, I'm calling out for help,
This is it—it clicks—I already know all too well!
I've been blessed with luck, with guides—
But not even my angels can see me through to the other side of THIS night,
And that's what I've missed, this IS on me,
There's only one way to get free, so here we go—
Hands to heart, gripping for life, I need to learn to march to only the beat inside,
HEAR ME, heart—we're fixing this—just KEEP BEAT-ING!
I need to stop thinking, stop the gears from turn-

ing,
WE'RE FIXING THIS!
Just keep beating;
First, I want to thank you, heart, for carrying this weight,
I've long-neglected you, but I'm here now—I'm listening!
Let's make some space, what do you have to say?
I let go—heaven knows surrender is the only true control;
Time dilates—now is eternal—I'm deep within, indifferent to the external,
I remember pre-consciousness—that pulsating pink bliss,
Memories rise of lives before this,
A culmination of bloodlines carrying pain through the ages,
Let's feel it all, what better time than now?
If surrender is salvation, let's die for myself;
JUST KEEP BEATING, HEART!
Finally this lion learns to bow to no other but himself,
The truth is clear—there's still this fear—
Not of death, but of unfinished work here,
So, what lingers—what threatens to stand in my way?

It's pain—grief and shame—
Wounds turned to scars, but memories remain,
Emotions were processed, but never released,
It's time to practice that inner alchemy—
Like never before,
My heart can't take much more,
So tight and heavy—but I'm down to my last—
So let's summon every drop of audacity I have;
I think of Blue, who went on but three years ago,
Not two feet from where my body now lies crum-
bled,
I remember her last breaths,
Feeling the cessation of air in her chest,
Light gone from her eyes, and I've said goodbye—
but I never let go,
The ones we love leave us, but that love *never* fol-
lows,
This can't mean carrying that sorrow for life—it's
just too heavy,
So I make the choice to let that pain go;
Thinking of Grammie, in that hospital room,
Machines beeping, and getting led away,
My only fear was born in that moment—
Afraid of loss, of words left unspoken,
That fear must go—

I accept I never had any control—of anything—
I surrender the grief of her and everyone in-be-
tween;
And right here, there it is—
I just want my dad—
I don't feel safe and I want to be protected,
A child cries within—I need to step up,
I must parent myself—become the guardian and the
guarded—
A balance of strength and love;
Tightness grips—
KEEP BEATING HEART—I'VE GOT THIS!
These are some mighty fine corners I've painted my-
self in!
I've got to remember—it's not what we carry—but
HOW we carry it!
Grief bled through tears, and pain absolved,
How long 'til I know if my gamble has paid off?
On the eleventh day—flashing lights came,
And vitals were high, until time began to un-dilate,
White-coats couldn't explain—but I knew very well
what had transpired,
And back home, I snipped that bracelet, and sleep
finally came,
And later that day, the sun was eclipsed,
I felt a rising inside—a phoenix reaching for bliss,

I didn't survive by chance or from medicines,
I stepped into my POWER—
And belief turned to wings, eclipsing the past—audacious transcendence.

Eden

Slowly but surely, the tide began to turn—and the destination became clear to anyone willing to see it.

The traveler was home.

Warmth—
Like July before age seven,
Like the sun tea mom left on the red table,
Pulling on my maroon shorts and tank,
When I was still barely able—
To dress myself—
And waiting quietly,
Drawing with crayons,
My own hands still so small—and yet unaware,
Of the worlds they would wield,
Of the darkness that would come to call;
Like a string between cans,
I call upon that child of sun—
Feet upon sand, hands up to tears—
Drying rivers of transmuted pain to power,
I was so old in those castles of youth,
I'm younger NOW, a child returns to walk in his truth.

Clinging Fire

Desire—coated in fire,
Burning through my heart,
Nature's con,
A species moves on—
Evolving to whatever's next,
What could have been—it scares me,
But I know better than to indulge such nonsense—
that's a past that doesn't exist;
Maddening—to be a conduit—
To accept what IS—
A glorious nightmare in the flesh,
To be in it so deep,
Knowing every PIECE of the whole is expendable,
Well a piece of ME is just not amenable—
To every soul's ambition—
Feeling like ammunition—never reaching closer
than an arm's length away—
What else can I say, when I know—
This is just a plot playing out,
No doubt heaven is just shaking itself out—
Through pieces of itself—
Having temporary flashes through shards of soul,
Oh, I know—all too well!

But knowledge can make the heart feel like a burn-
ing hell;
I long for the space beyond now,
I ache to know what it will feel like to step back out
of that bubble, once again—
Emerging as the truest form of my soul—
And to KNOW—TOUCH—as others speak of it,
To have this madness reciprocated until I choke on
it,
To laugh beside cinema people walking on by—lost
in the show,
A once-memory from so long ago,
And to KNOW—beyond a doubt—
What it would feel like, to be LIGHT,
To stop time in a loving embrace,
Feeling bliss separate from time and space,
As if I could see it all as both separate—AND part of
myself,
I've put myself through hell attempting to drive
away the hunger,
Better to get under it always eating at me—
Never reverse—
I accept these desires are just part of my ride
through this version of Earth,
Knowledge will never stop them from feeling like a
curse,

Unless I allow them to be only what they are—
Temporary charges—
I can't change fate any more than I could change a heart,
My now is here, accepting what is,
Burning inside, seeking oceans within—
Learning to walk through fire and to burn,
As I make my way home, as fire to the sun re-
turns.

Let it Burn

Mellow fiery defiance—
An arrested compliance,
Diving into caves—
Breaking chains, spitting—
Ashes of dying embers—
Beautiful death of false dimensions;
Ego lost to soul's intention,
Melancholy fire,
Accepting desire is just a conduit—
A catapulting mechanism—
For reaching new levels of bliss,
Awakening to heavens on new levels,

Channeled longing is a key to the plateau of Siddhic gift.

Insomnia creates a hole—
Collecting the drops of creation, of soul—
Which bleed in the silence,
Watering the winter's roots;

A fuller ghost, floating through space,
Timeless echoes on ear-drops of photons—
Echoes of stardust, flickers of grace,
Watching remnants of passers-by becoming one;

Just a dancing flame—
Waiting on the wind to take me on,
Fireflies collide where light divides—
Insomniac daydream was just a wish inside;

Now One, again—retreated from polarized ends,
Stardust falling onto fields in Eden, once again.

Observing the Observer

Silence echoed down the halls of his mind—the moment was upon him.

He'd made a choice earlier that year, and the time to set the wheels of action in motion had arrived; no longer could he stand with one foot in each world.

Storms had blown through, and as others projected their own fears upon him, he became acutely aware of the fact that his own fears had melted away entirely. As the last clouds dissipated, they drew the last remnants of fog along with them. The mirror he'd broken himself, so long ago, was once again whole. The familiar stranger gazed back at him. Everything clicked into place.

Looking out upon the harbour, he felt sadness for the world that was passing away. Of course a new one would arise in all its glory, but that imperfect battlefield had so much innate beauty—how could he not mourn its death throes?

He remembered everyone who'd gone on, and everyone he'd left alive, and knew the sting that would come when he closed the book. He would savour every moment—it was a blessing to have experienced in the flesh what so very few had.

He became the observatory itself, as the light waned—eager for the night—the long night that would lead to dawn.

About the Author

Hi, I'm Tyler! I'm a full-time writer and visual artist originally from just north of Boston, currently residing in Florida.

Writing began for me at age seven, as a form of therapy for dealing with the loss of my grandmother. It went from a near-constant lifelong hobby to a profession several years ago, when I took up ghost writing, and also began writing under several pen names. After a bad experience with ghost writing, I began releasing my own titles. "Parallel to Sundown" and "Static Flow" were my first poetry compilations. Walking Into Heaven is a natural follow-up.

More poetry is coming, along with a series of fiction-al novels and an autobiography. When not writing, you can usually find me with a camera in my hand, traveling as often as possible. My biggest loves are art and spending time with my family and close friends, including my cat, Catniss.

Also available:

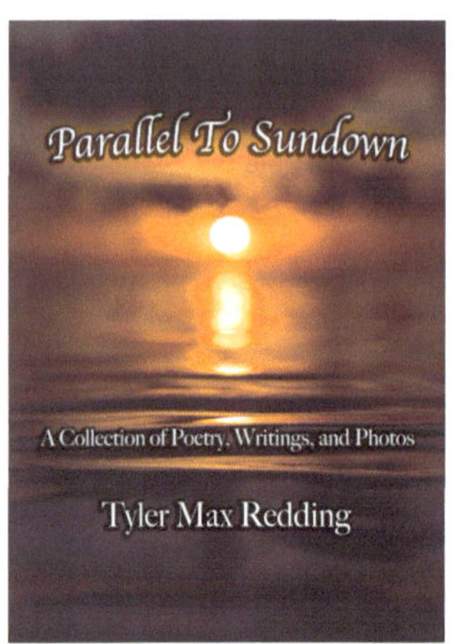

Let's connect!

linktree.com/tylerismaximus

Extended Photo Section

Self-mastery is all that can truly bridge these divides,
Go within, face that mirror full on,
Forget about all that lies outside;

The heart still beats from a seeming cage,
and all around the people keep moving...

Surrendering tides are salvation,

Truth in power negates expectation.

Scenes play out like cinema before our very eyes;
remember we watch from the director's chair.

In a cold world, one must become a perpetual
flame unto themself,

And suddenly, amidst the chaos, it hit him like a
thunderbolt that the storm was truly over. The tides
were turning, and none of it had been in vain. He cried
from the shock, he wanted to scream. He wouldn't
never be the same—that storm had erased everything
he was—but that was the entire point of the storm.

Love can drive even the most peaceful being to war.
Peace in itself, however, can open a higher door.

If you must cry out, then do it with such a ferocity that your very soul ignites, sending a beacon up through the night.

It was the pause, the space between the
words left unsaid that stung the most.

Everything must end—to begin again.

One moment can touch a soul;
one moment of defiance can shatter a mold;
one collective—touching down to take off—
stand tall, it's time to shake that mud off.

Just breathe, let it flow—
Everything revolves, even the birds know.

It was shortly before five in the morning as the man sat down on the wall next to the ocean. The sun was due to come up soon, and he slowly began snapping photos of the early dawn's light illuminating the waves, as the tide drifted out.

His mother had gone on ahead, down onto the sand below. He wanted to sit right here, alone—in silence—taking the moment in.

The sound of the waves was soothing, and the gradient of the sky was gradually shifting to pinks and oranges. He continued snapping the shutter of the camera, taking in the beauty around him. His mood was somber, but his surroundings provided solace and peace.

"Hello!"

The man was suddenly jolted from his peace by an unknown voice. He turned and saw a woman placing a black bag onto the wall behind him.

"Hey", he replied, spinning back around. He wasn't feeling social.

"Are you here taking pictures? I am too!"

He turned and glanced in her direction. He didn't

want to be rude, but he had exactly zero RAM for interacting with strangers. He turned back around, attempting to re-focus on the coming sunrise. Hopefully, the stranger would get the message.

"I just thought we could talk, since we're both taking photos. I guess you're not one of those kinds of people", she voiced, in a nasty tone.

He ignored her. Nothing was taking him out of this moment again. She wandered off.

He snapped some photos of his mother down on the sand, framed by the waves and the long-running wall. The sky was getting lighter. He took a couple long-exposures of the waves—they sounded so gentle. He began taking a video with his phone. The beautiful sound was once again interrupted by the obnoxious voice, talking over his video. The man couldn't make most of the words out over the sound of the waves, but as the complete stranger passed directly behind him, he did hear her telling him to "adjust his attitude."

A complete stranger, he thought. Who was she to pass any kind of judgement on him, or to feel entitled to his time or a conversation? He briefly considered telling her off, but no, he thought. She's just an NPC—a non-playable character—and she was only there to attempt to take him from his present moment. She gets ZERO explanation. Let her think whatever she wants.

What she couldn't possibly have known, was this day marked the fifth anniversary of his father's death. That every year, his mother brings a yellow rose to the beach at sunrise in memory of his father, and since he was home visiting—for the first twenty-fifth of June since his father passed, he'd gone along with his mother. He was grieving, in deeper ways than any year before, having just narrowly escaped death himself. He just wanted to take in the moment ALONE, in peace.

Think before you pass judgment on another person—you NEVER know what ANYONE is dealing with. If you can't spare the energy to be kind, just say nothing—as the man had attempted to do with the intrusive stranger. You are not entitled to anyone's time or energy. Check yourself—hold yourself accountable for your own actions. There is nothing and no one about this world that should bend to your demands—each and every person is but a piece of a whole.

Be kind, but if you can't be kind in the moment, at least don't be malicious. The world is tough enough already, let's not make it worse on each other.